DAS RELIGION

A Conservative Survival Manual for
Overcoming a Marxist America

DAS RELIGION

A Conservative Survival Manual for
Overcoming a Marxist America

RUSSELL HAMNER

LIBERTY HILL PRESS

Liberty Hill Press
2301 Lucien Way #415
Maitland, FL 32751
407.339.4217
www.libertyhillpublishing.com

Paperback ISBN-13: 978-1-6322-1318-1
Ebook ISBN-13: 978-1-6322-1319-8

Table of Contents

Introduction

T here is a war of ideology going in the US government: Liberal Democracy versus the Conservative Republican. Neither has fully proven itself, neither has disproved the other; thus arises the need to settle the argument.

Political theory is concerned with how we ought to live collectively, how power should be allocated, and to whom power should be allocated to best serve society. Theory helps equip us with the analytical tools necessary to differentiate between the legitimate functions of government and the arbitrary use of power.

This manual will compare the political theory of the liberal established welfare state against Christian charity to determine if the liberal welfare state is a legitimate function of government, or an arbitrary use of power in violation of the First Amendment.

The Argument

T he liberal established welfare state is a sham. The liberals have fraudulently usurped the charity model from Christianity and have established it as an arbitrary government function, which violates 83 percent[1] of US citizens' First Amendment rights and is banned by the Constitution.

Americans should be against the welfare state, Democratic socialism, and liberalism because they are all arbitrary and illegitimate political powers. They stand as a revival of the European overthrow of Christianity, where there is no separation of church and state.

This is the argument this book will attempt to prove beyond a reasonable doubt from here on out. Once people realize that they have been deceived, they are no longer deceived.

---

[1] Eighty-three percent of Americans identify themselves as Christians. ABC News analysis by Gary Langer http://abcnews.go.com/US/ story?id=90356&page=1

The Smoking Gun

I n 1968, the Social Security Administration commissioned Professor Theron Schlabach of the history department of Goshen College to examine the history and development of the Social Security Act. His report, *Rationality of Welfare: A Public Discussion of Poverty and Social Insurance in the United States 1875-1935*, was suppressed by the Social Security Administration for thirty-two years because it exposes the liberal takeover and government establishment of the Christian-based Charity Organization Societies, national establishments of welfare, healthcare, education, and housing created by Reverend Humphrey Gurteen in 1877.

Schlabach's first chapter of the report, titled "Charity a false start," and chapter two, titled "A Rationalization toward Welfare," depict the transition from religious control to government control. (I urge you to get a copy for your records from foot notes on page 5.)

The Charity Organization Societies were founded to further charity organizations by reforming them scientifically, assigning districts and training agents who would interview the prospective recipients of the charity to prevent the waste of energy, effort, and duplication of functions. Under Gurteen, the Charity Organization Societies had become part of the very structure of society. For the last quarter of the nineteenth century and into the 1930s, they were held as the conventional wisdom of American attitudes toward welfare.[2]

The Charity Organization Societies believed in relief and had been established to secure it, placing a high estimate on the educational and social values to provide any amount of assistance necessary to keep families together with "Care of Dependent Families and Their Homes," as the societies' slogan.

Around 1890, American elitists traveled to Europe for higher education. However, the European education in social politics the Americans learned had been developed from the church being part of the state, due to the Act of Supremacy of November 1534.

In an act of the Parliament of England under King Henry VIII, titled 26 Henry VIII c. 1, King Henry VIII declared that he was "the only supreme head on Earth of the Church of England" and that the English crown shall enjoy "all honors, dignities, preeminence's, jurisdictions, privileges, authorities, immunities, profits, and commodities to the said dignity."[3] This act established religion as a power of the state.

This seizure of power is the reason the constitutionalists left Europe for religious freedom, as well as the reason they penned the exact phraseology "Congress shall make no law respecting an establishment of religion, or prohibiting the free exercise thereof..." Due to these constitutionalists, although the government establishment of Christian welfare, healthcare, education,

---

[2] "Rationality and Welfare: Public Discussion of Poverty and Social Insurance in the United States 1875–1935." Chapter 1. http://www.socialsecurity.gov/history/reports/schlabach1.html

[3] Thurston, Herbert "Henry VIII." In Herbermann, Charles. Catholic Encyclopedia. New York: Robert Appleton Company. 1913.

and housing may still be legal in Europe, it is unconstitutional in the United States.[4]

Eventually, liberal progressives became reformers of charity and began advocating the European social insurance movement. In later years, notable literature was published on the subject. By 1893, John Graham Brooks provided Americans with their first detailed description of European social insurance.[5]

An expert on the staff of the United States Commissioner of Labor in the 1890s, and also an advocate of social insurance in 1898, William F. Willoughby wrote *Workingmen's Insurance*, in which he stated, "The modern movement for social insurance represented the effort to substitute for the old relief funds, which were too often founded upon a charitable basis."[6] This statement equates to the replacement of the Charity Organization Societies model from chapter 1 of Schlabach's report, with government-controlled insurance from chapter 2.

Other reformers used the same language, such as Charles R. Henderson, who wrote *Modern Methods of Charity,* stating, "Charity picked up the pieces when nothing else could be done. But something else could be done. Reformers had to find better

---

[4]   United States Constitution, First Amendment, United States Government Printing Office. Washington: 2007.

[5]   "Rationality and Welfare: Public Discussion of Poverty and Social Insurance in the United States 1875–1935." Chapter 1. http://www.socialsecurity.gov/history/reports/schlabach1.html

[6]   Schlabach, T. F. "Rationality and Welfare: Public Discussion of Poverty and Social Insurance in the United States 1875–1935." Chapter 2. 1969, referencing William Willoughby "Workingmen's Insurance." New York: 1898. http://www.socialsecurity.gov/history/reports/schlabach2.html.

solutions and embody them in statute law."[7] In this work, Henderson revealed their intent to make a law establishing religion.

In 1935, liberal-progressive president Franklin Delano Roosevelt did just that, introducing the Social Security Act to Congress, which sparked several rounds of litigation reaching the Supreme Court. Roosevelt's New Deal suffered multiple rulings that found it unconstitutional. However, none of these rulings considered the First Amendment. In a pivotal case in 1937, Supreme Court Justice Roberts changed his allegiance from the conservatives to the liberals, shifting the balance of the court from 5-4 against to 5-4 in favor. Roberts upheld previous unconstitutional decisions on minimum wage, including the National Labor Relations Act and the Social Security Act.[8]

Under Franklin Delano Roosevelt, the liberal-progressive party effectively usurped the religious charity organization model and substituted it with the Social Security Act's compulsion and taxing power. By doing so, Roosevelt transformed it to a law made by Congress respecting an establishment of religion in violation of the First Amendment.

In later years, the Supreme Court ruled that under the First Amendment, for a statute to be constitutional, the statute must have a secular, legislative purpose; secondly, its principal or primary effect must be one that neither advances nor inhibits religion (Board of Education v. Allen, 392 US 236, 243, 1968; [p613]). Finally, the statute must not foster "an excessive government

---

[7] Schlabach, T. F. "Rationality and Welfare: Public Discussion of Poverty and Social Insurance in the United States 1875–1935." Chapter 2. 1969, referencing Henderson's "Modern Methods of Charity." 507, NCCC Proceedings 599, 1906. http://www.socialsecurity.gov/history/reports/schlabach2.html

[8] https://www.ssa.gov/history/court.html. Supreme court decision history of Social Security Act.

entanglement with religion" (Walz, supra, at 674). The Social Security Act fails all three prongs. (I will share more on this later.)

This is the Supreme Court's interpretation of how the courts view First Amendment law, which might be effective in some but not all cases because they do not understand it is the Christian religion that requires a separation of religion and law, as the First Amendment rightly declares.

Biblical Separation Of Church And State

From the first century, the Christian religion has controlled the tenets of welfare, education, housing, and healthcare from the corporal acts of mercy, which deal with the physical body of a person, to feed the hungry, give drink to the thirsty, clothe the naked, shelter the homeless, visit those in prison, and relieve the sick.[9] This also includes the spiritual acts of mercy, which deal with the mental and emotional aspects of a person, such as to instruct the ignorant, to counsel the doubtful, to admonish sinners, to bear wrongs patiently, to forgive offences willingly, and to comfort the afflicted. The Christian communities who have established numerous institutions to carry out these duties widely understand the following precepts:

Education: college and university (5,037); elementary and secondary (59,327); libraries (6,863); research institutes (8,772); service and other (101,868); vocational, technical, and adult (6,651).

Healthcare: addiction and substance abuse (8,578); diseases and disease research (18,667); healthcare facilities and programs (53,769); medical disciplines and specialty research (5,794); mental health and crisis services (15,652).

---

[9]   Matthew 25:31-46 King James Version

Welfare: agriculture, food, and nutrition (10,811); crime and legal related (18,848); employment and occupations (15,353); general human services (131,330).

Housing: housing (35,920) public safety, disaster preparedness, and relief (18,637); recreation and sports (86,139); youth development (36,900). [10]

The government has never established anything; all they have done is use the law to assume all this power established by we the people.

The Christian acts of mercy originate from the time of Moses, when God came down on the mountain, after freeing Israel from Egypt, and gave Moses the two tables of stone called the Covenant, which Moses broke because the people violated it by worshiping the gold calf.

> "The Lord said unto Moses, hew thee two tables of stone like unto the first: and I will write upon these tables the words that were in the first tables, which thou brakest." [11] Further, God told Moses, "Write thou these words: for after the tenor of these words I have made a covenant with thee and with Israel." [12]

God wrote the Covenant on two stones, and Moses wrote the Covenant in the Pentateuch, which is recorded in Scripture as Leviticus, Numbers, and Deuteronomy.

Leviticus is the book of the Bible that contains instruction for the Levite priests. It shows the social side of God's divine

---

[10] https://www.guidestar.org/nonprofit-directory/religion/christian/1.aspx
Number of religious organizations under 501c3

[11] Exodus 34:1 King James Version

[12] Exodus 34:27-28 King James Version

natural law, which ordains the priests to care for the poor, be the doctors, and teach the people the religion and law. Jesus is the true Levite High Priest, who outlined the corporal acts of mercy from the social law of Leviticus in Matthew 25:31-46. In this passage, Jesus tells us to give drink to the thirsty, provide food to the hungry, clothe the naked, shelter the homeless, visit the sick, and visit those in prison.

Numbers contains a clause of the Covenant that separates the natural social law of Leviticus from the political legal law of Deuteronomy. This clause states that all the men from twenty years of age upward who are able to go to war for the legal government of Deuteronomy are to be separated and not permitted to execute any part of the social government of Leviticus.[13]

Deuteronomy is the book of the Bible that contains instructions for the legal government concerning laws for war, policing, and courts for execution of punishment.

God Himself created a separation between religion and government; therefore, the Christian religion requires a separation of religion and law. Thus, the Covenant of God is divine social and political science; Leviticus being the social science and Deuteronomy the political science. Numbers is the clause of the Covenant that separates the church of Leviticus from the state of Deuteronomy. Both have specific stipulations; Leviticus 1:3 states the Leviticus offerings must be done by free will, while Deuteronomy 1:3 states individuals are commanded to obey the law.

This religious model of social science brings a new understanding about how social, natural, and Levitical laws require free will and a separation from punitive law. This is because these laws rely on divine justice, with eternal life for those who obey.

Leviticus is the divine part of God's Covenant. Man understood the concept of penal law (being under the bondage of law in

---

[13] Numbers 1:47-54

Egypt), but because man had not known or understood divine law, God came, delivered, and performed the divine law of Leviticus miraculously to reveal its power to free man from the bondage of penal law.

Both God and Jesus performed the divine part of the Covenant as miracles to demonstrate the proper application of the corporal and spiritual acts of mercy. These acts of mercy are of the Holy Spirit, and Leviticus is the Holy Spirit written down. "Holy" means to be separate—in this case, separate from the law. In addition, miracles are the evidence of the Holy Spirit. The Bible shows these identical miracles in the Old Testament for God and in the New Testament for Jesus, as can be seen in the below examples:

> God gave drink to the thirsty by providing water from a rock: Old Testament, Exodus 17:6.

> Jesus gave drink to the thirsty by turning water into wine: New Testament, John 2:7-8. Jesus also offers living water: New Testament, John 4:14.

> God fed the hungry with manna from heaven: Old Testament, Exodus 16:15.

> Jesus fed the hungry when He fed five thousand, with only five loaves and two fish: New Testament, Matthew 14:17.

> God is the physician, as He kept Israel healthy forty years in the wilderness; even their clothes did not wear out: Old Testament, Deuteronomy 29:5; Nehemiah 9:21.

Jesus is the physician, as He healed the blind, the sick, the crippled, and the insane: New Testament, Matthew 9:27-29; Matthew 11:5; Matthew 4:23-24.

God went to those in prison, saving them from bondage in Egypt: Old Testament, Exodus 9:27-33.

Jesus went to those in prison, opening the gates of prison and breaking the shackles off Peter: New Testament, Acts 12:10-17.

It was God's will to free Israel from bondage, as well as to feed, give drink, clothe, house [give land], and heal them. Jesus did the will of God, and God raised Him from the dead. Jesus educates the church to believe in Him and to do the corporal acts of mercy, as He and God did, and He will give them eternal life. Matthew 25:31-46 states the following:

> [31]When the son of man shall come in his Glory, and all the holy angels with him, then he shall sit upon the throne of his glory:

Jesus is with the disciples speaking of His second coming, telling all that He will require and expect from the church upon His arrival the next time.

> [32]And before him shall be gathered all nations: and he shall separate them one from another, as a shepherd divideth his sheep from his goats:

> [33]And he shall set the sheep on his right hand, but the goats on his left.

Now, Jesus sits on the right hand of God, and He sets the sheep on His right, then it places them under His saving authority. And, if He places the goats on His left, He places them between He and His Father's authority, set for judgment.

> [34] Then shall the king say unto them on his right hand, Come. You blessed of my Father, inherit the Kingdom prepared for you from the foundation of the world.

> [35] For (because) I was an hungred and you gave me meat: I was thirsty, and you gave me drink: I was a stranger, and you took me in:

> [36] Naked and you clothed me: I was sick, and you visited me: I was in prison and you came unto me.

As you have seen, these are the miracles God and Jesus did, for this He said unto them, "Come you blessed of my Father, inherit the kingdom prepared for you from the foundation of the world."[14]

> [37] Then shall the "righteous" answer him, saying Lord, when saw we thee an hungred, and fed thee? Or thirsty and gave thee drink?

> [38] When saw we thee a stranger, and took thee in? or naked and clothed thee?

> [39] Or when saw we thee sick, or in prison, and came unto thee?

---

[14] Matthew 25:34

The sheep are now called the righteous because they have done the righteousness explained in verses 35 and 36. When you understand that care for the poor is the righteousness that God and Jesus did in their miracles, you can finally understand what it means to be born again. First John 2:29 says, "If you know he is righteous, ye know that everyone that doeth righteousness is born of him."

> [40] and the King shall answer and say unto them, Verily I say unto you, inasmuch as you have done it unto the least of these my brethren, you have done it unto me.

Herein lies the personal relationship with Jesus: He did righteousness. You did righteousness; therefore, you are born unto Him. As His child, you have spiritually done it to Him. Those who have not done righteousness to Him are not born unto Him, even though He did it to them.

> [41] Then shall he say also unto them on the left hand, Depart from me, you cursed, into everlasting fire, prepared for the devil and his angels:
>
> [42] For I was an hungred, and you gave me no meat: I was thirsty, and you gave me no drink:
>
> [43] I was a stranger, and you took me not in: naked, and you clothed me not: sick, and in prison, and you visited me not.
>
> [44] Then shall they also answer him, saying, Lord, when saw we thee an hungred, or athirst, or a

stranger, or naked, or sick, or in prison, and did not minister unto thee?

[45] Then shall he answer them, saying, Verily I say unto you, inasmuch as you did it not to one of the least of these, you did it not to me.

[46] And these shall go away into everlasting punishment: but the righteous into life eternal.

From these verses, you can see that if you believe in Jesus for eternal life, you <u>must</u> believe His instructions to enter eternal life over what the world has told you about how to enter eternal life. It is also important to know that righteousness is giving life.

God and Jesus both did righteousness; therefore, Jesus was born unto God, and God raised Him from the dead with eternal life. If you do righteousness, as Jesus did, you are born unto Him, and you too will have life eternal.

The Bible states that you must forgive to be forgiven,[15] and if you live by the sword, you must also die by the sword.[16] The same is so with life everlasting—you must give life to be given life, and when you do not give life, life cannot be given to you. God is the giver of life and all that is necessary for life; and Jesus came that we might have life more abundantly.[17] The Holy Spirit is the Spirit of life and giving life more abundantly.

For this reason, Jesus said, "Seek ye first the kingdom of God and his righteousness, and all these things will be added unto

---

[15] Mark 11:26

[16] Revelation 13:10

[17] John 10:10

you."[18] For the kingdom of God is righteousness and joy in the Holy Spirit.[19]

It is impossible for the miracles of God and Jesus Christ to be secular, (Non religious) for they are the root and branch of Christianity. Without these works of mercy from Leviticus, of which Jesus is king, there is no Christianity

An argument then arises as to the political nature of the welfare state when those policies are the miracles of God and Jesus Christ. Secondly, another argument arises as to the secular nature of the welfare state, such as when Jesus stated, "When you care for the least of these, you have done it to me," creating a personal relationship with Him in the struggle for the kingdom of God. Lastly, a third argument arises as to the secular nature of the welfare state, concerning how Jesus defined the corporal acts of mercy as the central tenets of religion. He stated that those who did them receive eternal life, fulfilling the ultimate purpose of religion: life everlasting.

From the beginning of time, God created a separation between religion and government; thus, the constitutionalists were not the force that created the separation by government power. It is the Christian religion that requires a separation of church and state. Further, doing the acts of mercy by force of law negates the Covenant and, in turn, eternal life.

"Therefore, by the deeds of the law there shall no flesh be justified in his sight:"[20] This is because one did not do righteousness by free will, as required by Leviticus 1:3; rather, one did righteousness by force of law.

---

[18] Matthew 6:33

[19] Romans 14:7

[20] Romans 3:20

The Covenant is the basis of religion and religious under-standing. It is the starting point to understanding religion, from which all Scripture flows. The Christian religion began when God came to earth and gave the Levitical laws; it is common knowledge that Leviticus was written for the Levites, who were the priests.

From the beginning, when God gave the Covenant of Leviticus, He simultaneously gave the law of Deuteronomy. Now that the law was given at the time of the Covenant, this brought much confusion, so much that Leviticus, along with Deuteronomy, was collectively called the Law of Moses. Moreover, under the law of Deuteronomy, religious leaders punished citizens for failure to uphold the law of Leviticus, despite the fact that Levitical law was to be done by free will, and followers should have the conscience to obey or not obey it without punishment of law.

Therefore, it was necessary for God to send the prophets to instruct the leaders toward the kingdom of God by obedience to the Covenant. To some, He gave the inspiration by dreams or visions, such as Nebuchadnezzar or Solomon. For certain prophets, God sent direct contact with angelic beings, such as Daniel.

In Malachi, the religious leaders had become corrupt by offering blind and lame sacrifices[21] when they had healthy males to offer.[22] They also were to be teachers of the law and religion and had become corrupt in that as well by perverting law and religion.[23]

Finally, because the religious leaders would not repent from perverting law and religion, God states in Malachi that He will send the messenger of the Covenant and will give a New Covenant in their hearts.[24] When Jesus, the King of Leviticus, arrived, He

---

[21] Malachi 1:8

[22] Malachi 1:14

[23] Malachi 2:8

[24] Malachi 3:1

performed the miracles that God had done in Exodus, but left out the performing or using of Deuteronomy law.

This can be seen in John 8:1-12, which tells of a woman caught in the act of adultery. The Jews tried to get Jesus to stone her based on the law of Deuteronomy, but Jesus refused and forgave the woman from Levitical law.

The New Covenant is the Old Covenant without the law of Deuteronomy. God raised Jesus from the dead to prove that Leviticus was the only way to salvation and that Deuteronomy was not necessary for salvation.

The constitutionalists formed the United States of America on the principles set forth in Leviticus and Deuteronomy, and implemented a separation of church and state in the Constitution's First Amendment from the clause of the Covenant in Numbers. The constitutionalists carefully worded the First Amendment to separate religion from law. Instructing: "Congress (the lawmakers) shall make no law respecting an establishment of religion, nor prohibiting the free exercise thereof."[25]

If Congress makes a law concerning religion, it establishes that power as government duty. Secondly, if Congress makes a law-respecting religion, it then becomes a law and is no longer free will, in violation of Leviticus 1:3, which also violates the free exercise retained in the First Amendment's free exercise clause.

The First Amendment also makes it constitutional for religion to establish the national temple, separate from the national government, as is required by the Covenant. Moreover, religion must be free from government making laws for or against it. Religion has its own sovereignty of natural law, which is both equal to and separate from political government's sovereignty of punitive law.

---

[25] First Amendment to the Constitution

The Great Seal - Foundations Of Religious Freedom

T he Great Seal is the evidence that the constitutionalists acknowledged religion's sovereignty.

On July 4, 1776, after writing the Declaration of Independence, Congress passed a resolution. Congress appointed Benjamin Franklin, James Adams, and Thomas Jefferson to create the Great Seal of the United States; proposed to reflect the beliefs and values that the founding fathers established in the Declaration of Independence and attached to the new nation, which they wished to pass on to their posterior.[26]

A lengthy description of the meaning of the eagle side was given by the committee, but they left the pyramid side of the seal an unexplained mystery. In my studies, I have found the Great Seal is a parable of symbols, and to understand the meaning of the seal, you must understand the origin of the parable.

We all understand the eagle side of the seal is the symbol for the national government. It depicts the national coat of arms of the United States. The coat of arms is used on official documents of the federal government, and the seal of the President of United States is based directly on the Great Seal.[27]

---

[26] US Dept. of State, Bureau of Public Affairs, "The Great Seal," page six.

[27] US Dept. of State, Bureau of Public Affairs, "The Great Seal," page 7-9.

The pyramid side of the seal is referred to as the "spiritual side of the seal."[28] This can be seen on the back of the one-dollar bill, which shows an unfinished pyramid with the Latin phrase "Annuit Coeptis" above the pyramid and "Novus Ordo Seclorum" below. There are many conspiracy theories about the pyramid side of the seal, ranging from the Masons to the Illuminati taking over the world spread across the internet, which should be put to rest. I believe that most of these theories were formed from people not understanding the meaning, and are based on speculation to which I will attempt to debunk.

The pyramid exists as a reflection of the colonists' dilemma, who were making an exodus from Europe for religious freedom. Where would a Christian look for guidance in making an exodus for religious freedom but the biblical book of Exodus, where God gave the instructions to Moses to leave Egypt so they could worship Him. Geographically, the symbol of the pyramid is a symbol of Egypt, a reminder of the time of Exodus when God freed the Israelites so they could freely worship Him.

The all-seeing eye atop of the pyramid is a reminder of the time of Exodus when God came down on the mountain and gave His divine providence, personally handing Moses the Covenant on the two stone tablets recorded in Leviticus and Deuteronomy.

The delta (Δ) is a mathematical symbol of change, as well as a symbol that represents Jesus as the Chief cornerstone of the Temple. The pyramid is also known as the "temple of kings," which represents Leviticus, the Temple, and ultimately, Jesus. It was also a religious symbol for the Egyptians entering life everlasting.

The ray of light surrounding the delta signifies intellectual freedom given by God in the Covenant. The Roman numerals totaling 1776 at the base of the pyramid are representative of the

---

[28] US Dept. of State, Bureau of Public Affairs, "The Great Seal," page six.

year when the constitutionalists laid the foundation for the separation of church and state.

The Declaration of Independence describes the God-given right to establish a national temple, as well as the government of law expressed in the Great Seal, stating, "To have a nation with the separate and equal station which the laws of nature (in Deuteronomy) and nature's God entitle them"[29] (in Leviticus).

Then you will notice that the pyramid is unfinished, symbolizing that the temple is unfinished, for we have no national temple yet.

The Great Seal also includes two Latin phrases: "ANNUIT COEPTIS" and "NOVUS ORDO SECLORUM."

"ANNUIT COEPTIS" means "God has approved," signifying that God has approved our undertakings.[30] Certainly, God has approved the establishment of the Covenant with the national temple for social justice, guarded by the First Amendment. He has also approved the national government for defense, guaranteed by Article 4 § 4 in the Constitution. God has approved the establishment of His Covenant, as He has designed it and handed it to mankind in Exodus, which Jesus confirmed by saying, "Thy kingdom come, thy will be done," in Matthew 6:10.

"NOVUS ORDO SECLORUM" means "New Age Order," or "New Order of the Ages.[31]" This refers to the end times and the end of the world age. This order will be fulfilled when we obey the Covenant on earth as is in heaven. Furthermore, this action will begin the new age order of the kingdom of God.

This order fulfills the prayer of Christ: "Thy kingdom come, thy will be done, on earth as is in heaven" (Matt. 6:10). Also, the

---

[29] The Declaration of Independence

[30] https://greatseal.com/mottoes/seclorum.html

[31] https://greatseal.com/mottoes/seclorum.html

order fulfills Daniel's end-time prophecy, which states, "In the days of these kings shall God of heaven set up a kingdom, which shall never be destroyed" (Dan. 2:44).

The New Order also refers to the United States being the first step of Revelation 11:15, in which the kingdoms of this world have become the kingdoms of our Lord [Supreme Judge of the world] and His Christ [Supreme Priest of this world].

To conclude, on the opposite side of the seal, the eagle stands as another reminder of Exodus, which is found in Exodus 19:4-6. This passage describes the terms of the Covenant.

> You have seen what I did to the Egyptians: [punished by Deuteronomy law], and how I bare you on "eagles wings" and brought you unto myself [saved by Leviticus law]. Now therefore, if ye will obey my voice indeed, and keep my covenant, then ye shall be a peculiar treasure unto me above all people: for all the earth is mine:
>
> And ye shall be unto me a "<u>Kingdom</u>" of priests, and an holy nation. These are the words, which thou shalt speak unto the children of Israel.[32]

Thus, God leaves it to humankind to complete our part of the Covenant by establishing the kingdom of priests, as well as the government of law which He created, also known as the kingdom of God, by obedience to the Covenant.

---

[32] Exodus 19:4-6

The First Amendment
– Foundations Of
Constitutional Law

Together, the Great Seal, the Declaration of Independence, and the Constitution echo the privilege God has afforded to humankind to establish His kingdom.

As I explained in the previous chapter, the constitutionalists created the Great Seal as visible evidence of a sovereign nation and a free people with high aspirations and grand hope for the future.[33] On the seal, they included the pyramid as the symbol of a national temple of religion's natural divine law, governed by free will. This symbol is equal to but separate from the eagle, the symbol of a national legislative and defense body, governed by force of law.

The Declaration of Independence speaks of our God-given rights to assume the powers of the earth, a separate and equal station under the laws of nature and nature's God entitle them. As we have seen, God entitles us to have a national temple, shown by the pyramid on the seal, and a national government shown by the eagle side of the seal.

The Constitution is the establishment of Deuteronomy, shown by the eagle on the Great Seal, which was separately established in

---

[33] US Dept. of State, Bureau of Public Affairs, "The Great Seal," p. 6.

1787. Then in 1789, Congress proposed the first ten amendments, which were added in 1791. The first ten amendments begin with the separation of religion and law, which is expressed in the First Amendment, ending with the Tenth Amendment, separating the powers of the national government from the powers of the state government, as well as separating the powers of the federal and state government from the powers of we the people.[34]

In biblical terms, the powers of the federal and state governments would be from Deuteronomy, and the powers of we the people (the congregation) would be from Leviticus.

To take our country back from the liberal stranglehold, you must first take back religion. The liberals have sunk their hooks into the voters by using the welfare state as a method of payment for votes, promising more welfare benefits to those who vote to get them elected, which is illegal.

> Whoever makes or offers to make an expenditure to any person, either to vote or withhold his vote, or to vote for or against any candidate. And Whoever solicits, accepts, or receives any such expenditure in consideration of his vote or the withholding of his vote — Shall be fined under this title or imprisoned not more than one year, or both; and if the violation was willful, shall be fined under this title or imprisoned not more than two years, or both.[35]

---

[34] https://www.whitehouse.gov/about-the-white-house/the-constitution/

[35] 18 USC, sec. 597, Expenditures to Influence Voting.

The Unconstitutional Nature Of Liberal-Progressivism

I n the clearly established First Amendment law, Lemon v. Kurtzman 403 US 602 (1971), the Supreme Court has stated that first, the statute must have a secular legislative purpose:

The Social Security Act, the Affordable Healthcare Act, the Housing and Urban Development Act, and the Education Act do not have secular purposes when they are the establishment of the Christian-controlled Levitical corporal and spiritual acts of mercy, aka charity. Secondly, its principal or primary effect must be one that neither advances nor inhibits religion (Board of Education v. Allen, 392 US 236, 243, 1968).

The primary effects of the Social Security Act, the Education Act, the Housing and Urban Development Act, and the Affordable Healthcare Act advance religion's welfare, healthcare, education, and housing efforts and inhibit the free exercise thereof. Finally, the statute must not foster "an excessive government entanglement with religion" (Walz, supra, at 674).

The Social Security Act, the Education Act, the Housing and Urban Development Act, and the Affordable Healthcare Act create an excessive entanglement with religion where government controls a two-trillion-dollar market share, compared to religion's 427-billion-dollar market share.

The general rule is that an unconstitutional statute, though having the form and name of law, is in reality no law; rather, it is wholly void and ineffective for any purpose, since the unconstitutionality dates from the time of its enactment. In legal contemplation, an unconstitutional law is inoperative, as if it had never been passed (16Am. Jur 2d Sec 177 late sec 256).

Since an unconstitutional law is void, the general principles follow that this "law" imposes no duties, confers no rights, creates no office, bestows no power or authority to anyone, affords no protection, and justifies no acts performed under it. A void act cannot be legally consistent with a valid one. Therefore, an unconstitutional law cannot operate to supersede any existing valid law. Insofar as a statute runs counter to the Constitution, it is thereby superseded.

Strictly speaking, an unconstitutional law is not a law, nor should it be called a law, even if a court sustains it; for a finding that an unconstitutional statute is constitutional does not make it so.

Consequently, the First Amendment to the law of the land supersedes the Social Security Act, the Affordable Healthcare Act, the Housing and Urban Development Act, and the Education Act. In turn, these acts are constitutionally invalid. Therefore, the duties they create are invalid, the rights they infer are invalid, the offices they establish are invalid, the power and authority they infer are invalid, and the government protection and justification they claim are invalid.

Since the time of Moses, the act of caring for the poor, education, and healthcare has been the duty, right, power, and authority of the Judeo-Christian religion.

The liberal-progressive agenda that has become so common among American citizens today has tragically overlooked the constitutional foundations established in the First Amendment and the economic effects of their own unfounded claims.

While the liberal-progressive ideology infers that the welfare state is good for the economy, the Joint Economic Committee studies strongly refute that assertion.

For example, for every one dollar of federal welfare state spending curtailed, the economy will expand $1.38 in the same year. In other words, every dollar of federal restraint produces an economic value of $0.38. The failure to do so results in a net reduction in economic growth of $0.38. If this is maintained over the course of seven years, the economic output would increase to $2.45 for every dollar of restraint enacted in the first year and sustained through the period.[36]

In addition to this unfounded assertation, the liberal-progressive ideology also infers that the welfare state is good for the working people, yet the Joint Economic Committee studies strongly refute this as well.

In essence, every one dollar of welfare state spending curtailed would yield an increase of $0.26 in total wages, which amounts to $1.68 over the course of seven years. If federal welfare state spending had been held at its constant 1965 percent of GDP, the present value of gains to the typical worker over twenty years would net $106,800.00, enough to purchase a median-priced home.[37]

The philosophy of liberal progressivism also infers that the welfare state benefits middle-class families; once again, the Joint Economic Committee studies nullify this statement.

Families headed by adults between the ages of twenty-five and thirty-four lose an average of $1,418.00 a year for every $100 billion increase in welfare state spending. Every $100 billion

---

[36] Joint Economic Committee Study 1, Jim Saxton, Vice chairman, 1996, *"The Impact of the welfare state on the American economy,* page 1.

[37] Joint Economic Committee Study 2, Jim Saxton, Vice chairman, 1996, *"The Impact of the welfare state on workers,* page 1.

restrained from welfare state spending would increase the median family income by $895.00.[38]

Also, liberal progressives infer that the welfare state is advantageous for children, while the Joint Economic Committee refutes this belief.

For every $33,000.00 in federal non-defense spending, one less child would grow up in poverty. The restraint of $100 billion in non-defense spending lowers the child poverty rate by 4.35 percent, which would reduce the number of children in poverty by 3 million.[39]

These are the real-time, ruinous effects of unconstitutionally establishing and enforcing natural-social Levitical law by Deuteronomy positive law. The very heart of the liberal-progressive argument is counterproductive, where the effects of the welfare state do the opposite of what they have intended.

Essentially, the liberal-progressive inference that the welfare state is constitutional is based solely on two words in the Constitution: *general welfare*.

The liberal progressive interprets Article 1 § 8 term general welfare to be about the welfare state; however, the Constitution supports the interpretation as *safety*.

Article 4 § 4 States: "The United States shall guarantee to every state in this Union a Republican form of Government and shall protect every state from invasion." This confirms that Article 1 § 8 term general welfare allows taxation for the common defense to protect from invasion as *safety*.

Article 4 § 4 continues, "Upon Application of the Legislature, or the executive branch the United States shall protect every state

---

[38] Joint Economic Committee Study 5, Jim Saxton, Vice chairman, 1996, *"The Impact of the welfare state on the American family,* page 1.

[39] Joint Economic Committee Study 3, Jim Saxton, Vice chairman, 1996, *"The Impact of the welfare state on the children,* page 1.

from domestic violence." This confirms that Article 1 § 8 term "General welfare" allows taxation for defense from domestic violence as *safety*. [40]

The Constitution does not support the liberal-progressive interpretation that government has a duty to care for the poor or to provide healthcare, education, and housing. The Constitution does not delegate social power to the United States. Society is not government or state. The federal government, state government, and society are three separate and distinct bodies. Consequently, the Tenth Amendment reserves social power to society, as it states in pertinent part:

"The powers not delegated to the United States by the constitution, nor prohibited by it to the states, are reserved to the states respectively, or to the people."[41]

The social powers of religious welfare, healthcare, education, and housing are not delegated to the United States, but are banned to the federal government in the First Amendment. They are also banned to the states in the First Amendment, applicable via incorporation through the Fourteenth Amendment, which states, "No State shall make or enforce any law which shall abridge the privileges or immunities of citizens of the United States."[42]

This amendment was added to expressly prohibit the States from violating the immunities and privileges of the citizens in the Constitution's Bill of Rights, in which the First Amendment was focused on Congress.

Therefore, all social and religious rights are reserved to the people.

---

[40] The United States Constitution

[41] Tenth Amendment, United States Constitution

[42] Fourteenth Amendment, United States Constitution

When religious social science models prove government social science hypotheses untrue, it is logical then that government social science is untrue, refuted science. Additionally, when there is a true, religious, social science model whose hypothesis proves to be true, then it is logically the true social science model.

Religion's natural law of charity has a real purpose built into reality. The liberal-progressive usurpation of this natural law has no place, because that place has already been rightfully filled. Even reality rejects the liberal-progressive premises, which can be examined by liberal policies resulting in the opposite of what was intended.

The Bondage Of Liberal Political Ideologies And The Freedom Of Religion

rom the time of Moses, some 3,400 years ago, when God gave His divine social political science, humanity has searched for the answer of how and to whom to allocate power to best serve a nation.

Man has given his best shot. Plato, Aristotle, Socrates, and Aquinas were all great philosophers who had some good ideas, but they lacked complete theories because they all lacked the knowledge of God and the nature of man.

Liberalism, progressive socialism, and communism have become the rejection of religion, conservatism, and capitalism, as well as God and His nature. All these ideologies came from philosophers in Europe, where there is no separation of church and state. They have been framed from the conscience that the church is part of the state power, which is the foundational belief for these ideologies. They did not have to question if they violate the US Constitution. Even though they have infiltrated the US today, no European social-political theories have succeeded in supplanting or replacing the Christian Covenant of separation of church and state or the Constitution's First Amendment separating religion from law.

Therefore, all European social-political theories born out of a theory that there is no separation of religion and law violate the First Amendment's declaration that "Congress shall make no law respecting an establishment of religion, nor prohibiting the free exercise thereof,"[43] and any establishment of those theories are unconstitutional.

The liberal-progressive ideology amounts to bondage under the law; where you are already legally bound to punitive law, you are now also legally bound to social and natural law, as if it were punitive law, meaning there is only one sphere of freedom left: what you think in your mind.

This all started with Karl Marx, or at least he is the go-to philosopher that has fueled the world with placing people under the bondage of law.

Karl Marx (1818-1883) said, "If I dethrone God, then I also dethrone the king who reigns by the grace of God."[44]

Marx's social writings reveal undeniable hostile parallels with Scripture, which is intended as a deliberate replacement meant to expunge Christianity from society. Marx also opined that capitalism would eventually become unsustainable and would be replaced with socialism.[45] Being one of the first to coin the term "socialism," Marx never conceived a separation of religion from law.

On what authority does the Left rest? On Marx, a man who was born into this world knowing nothing, like all of us, who lived under government seizure of religion and the bondage of law from birth?

---

[43] First Amendment, United States Constitution

[44] Revelations concerning the communist trial in Cologne, Marx, 1853.

[45] The **Communist Manifesto**, written by Karl **Marx** and Friedrich **Engels**, February 21, 1848,

Karl Marx's social political theories spawned the greatest number of murders under one cause in the history of civilization. By looking at history, we can see the effects of his philosophies:

Under Mao Zedong, Marxist revolutionary (1893-1976), 45 million died.

Under Joseph Stalin, Marxist revolutionary (1879-1953), 14 million died.

Under Vladimir Lenin, Marxist revolutionary (1870-1924), 6-10 million died.

Under Adolph Hitler, Marxist revolutionary (1889-1945), 12 million died.[46]

In most of these cases, the first to go always seemed to be the religious who objected because they threatened the Marxist social power.

Similarly, the creed of modern-day extremist Muslims is to have government-controlled religion under Sharia law, which uses the power of political government to kill the infidel for religious reasons of not agreeing with a murderous totalitarian religion. However, Sharia law is unconstitutional in the United States, as it is a law-establishing religion and is therefore in violation of the First Amendment.

In the United States, the liberal-progressive movement dons itself as caring and compassionate, but in reality, it has seized religion's role and made it punitive law, using it to ostracize the religious in an effort to expunge religion from society.

In 1837, Horace Mann, as a member of the US House of Representatives in Massachusetts 8th district, became an education reformer, seizing religion's power of education from the spiritual acts of mercy and establishing it as government power. Then, by

---

[46] 1994, R. J. Rummel's book *Death by Government*

1962, under government power, liberal progressives stopped all religious discourse in education under the Education Act.[47]

Now, fifty-eight years later, the liberal-progressive ideology continues to evince a design to use the power of government to stamp out God and religion from society.

This is what I am talking about when I say that we are under bondage of law. The liberal-progressives seized the power of religion, then slowly make it illegal; it is insidious. They unconstitutionally made education a government duty, then said, "Wait a minute; it is a violation of the First Amendment for government to teach religion because of the separation of church and state, and as good Americans, we must all obey the Constitution."

"By the law is the knowledge of sin."[30] This means that the law legally commits sin. The criminal murders the victim; the law premeditatedly kills the criminal. Ergo, the law is the knowledge of sin and, in turn, is imperfect in bringing peace.

The divine law of religion is without the knowledge of sin; it does not force, coerce, threaten, or punish. "The fruit of the Spirit is love, joy, peace, longsuffering, gentleness, goodness, faith, meekness, temperance: against such, there is no law.[48] Love works no ill to his neighbor: therefore, love is the fulfilling of the law."[49]

God created religion to be the divine counterpart to government, to offset the damages a capitalist government has caused, such as potentially placing the weaker into poverty. God would not be God if He did not understand all political systems and then provide the science to have peace. God created Levitical law to save us from the damages caused by all imperfect political systems,

---

[47] https://www.pewforum.org/2019/10/03/religion-in-the-public-schools-2019-update/

[48] Galatians 5:22-23

[49] Romans 13:10

such as socialism, communism, Muslimism, and even capitalism. Political systems were not called by these names in Egypt, but their effects still bring bondage under the law.

Religion's free exercise of charity, being welfare, healthcare, and education cannot cause bondage where it is brought about by free will, without coercion of law. Free will is the superior system that allows one's conscience to choose without fear of punishment for what one believes. The free will secured through religion's separation from law protects us from socialism, communism, and radical Muslimism.

Liberty is freedom from arbitrary or despotic government or control. The liberal-progressive welfare state is arbitrary law and is becoming a despotic weapon used to war against religion, conservatism, and capitalism; this weapon is dividing our country and disrupting government progress.

As previously stated, the liberal progressives have taken over education and prohibited religious discourse in the schools under the Education Act, and they are now educating our children to know only liberalism: they don't teach the Constitution, religion, or history, for they know these aspects of the nation shine the light of truth against their cause.

Fortunately, God knows the damages of liberalism and desires that we are set free from it. All end-time prophecy is based on the end of man's form of government and the beginning of the kingdom of God. The kingdom shall not be left to others but shall break into pieces and consume all other kingdoms. It shall stand forever.[50]

As I have previously explained, the Great Seal of the United States testifies to this prophecy, stating, "Annuit Ceoptis," which means "God has approved." Essentially, God has approved the separation of church and state. The seal also states, "Novus Ordo

---

[50] Daniel 2:44

Seclurum," or "New Age Order," referring to the order of the kingdom of God.

When we wake up to the fact that the pyramid is the national symbol of religion and the eagle is the national symbol of the government, which together symbolize the kingdom of God, we can finally solve the puzzle of social and political science.

Malachi is the last book written before the advent of Jesus Christ; many today believe we are in the generation of the last days, leading to the second advent.

In Malachi, the priests were teaching the people wrongly about the law and the Covenant by not having a separation of religion and law. God gave the priests one last chance to repent and told them what would happen if they repented and brought all the tithes into the temple. This is also an example of what God will do when we obey the Covenant.

> Bring all the tithes into the storehouse so there will
> be meat in my house and prove me now herewith if
> I will not open the windows of heaven and pour out
> a blessing that there shall not be room enough to
> receive it.[51] And I will rebuke the devourer for your
> sakes, and he shall not destroy the fruits of your
> ground; neither shall your vine cast her fruit before
> the time in the field, saith the LORD of hosts.[52]

As you can see in this example, there is not one word about the law, only religion.

When you unravel it, this is the most profound statement in the Bible. In today's language, this would mean bringing all the

---

[51] Malachi 3:10

[52] Malachi 3:11

tithes into the temple, essentially, doing what God said to do in the Covenant; and by doing so, you would see for yourself if He would not open the windows of heaven and pour you out a blessing so immense that there would not be enough room to receive it. And He would rebuke the devourer and heal our land.[53]

Further, if we do this and God does what He said He would do, it will prove there is a God once and for all. Let God be true but every man a liar.[54]

---

[53] Malachi 3:11

[54] Romans 3:4

Liberal Influence And The
Remedy Of A National Church

Many people understand the functions of government, the Constitution, and the Bill of Rights, to some degree, but few, if any, understand the function of the church.

At any time, you can turn on the TV, tune in to the religious channel, and watch what the leaders have been taught about religion. If you pay attention, you will see they do not understand that the separation of church and state is a separation of religion and law—religion being the church, and the state being a government of laws. They do not understand the following:

- They do not understand the kingdom of God from the perspective of God and Jesus.
- They do not understand righteousness from the perspective of God and Jesus.
- They do not understand being born again from the perspective of God and Jesus.
- They do not understand salvation from the perspective of God and Jesus.

These religious leaders do not understand these important truths because they have learned religion from the liberal progressives, who took over academia and religion in the United States.

Under the Education Act, the liberal progressives have taken over every primary and secondary school in the United States. They make the curriculum; you will learn what they want you to learn, and they teach liberalism, progressivism, and socialism. They have also taken over higher education, as virtually all professors today are liberal-progressive gatekeepers.

The liberal progressives turn your children into snowflakes that melt under any pressure that deviates from liberal progressivism. Under the blindfolds of liberalism, capitalism, and religion have become hate speech that drives American students into safe spaces where they are protected from the First Amendment's freedom of speech.

Robert Kiyosaki's book *Fake Teachers, Fake Money, Fake Assets* reveals how the lies of teachers are making the poor and middle class poorer. Building a reserve-culture to support the welfare state, they hate the rich, knowing the rich do not support the welfare state.

This is ever present with President Trump; liberals hate him because he is rich and he is not a liberal progressive. For liberals, it's okay that Bernie Sanders, the Clintons, Joe Biden, and George Soros are rich, simply because they are liberal progressives. They want President Trump to show his tax returns because they know the average American does not know citizens do not pay taxes on real estate investments. And they would use it to try and destroy him.

James Madison said, "I cannot undertake to lay my finger on the article of the Constitution which granted a right to Congress of expending, on objects of benevolence, the money of their constituents."[55] In other words, there is no constitutional provision

---

[55] Annuls of Congress, House of Representatives, 3rd Congress 1st session, page 170, (1794-01-10).

for government to spend tax monies on charity, care for the poor, kindness, equality, income redistribution, or socialism.

The liberal progressive ideology has educated average Americans to believe they are patriots solely because they pay taxes. Now "I am a patriot who pays his taxes" has become a common saying.

In the United States, 155 million people are working and paying taxes to support 200 million who do not work and pay taxes, so are the 200 million non-patriots? Of course not; they are the liberal-progressive poster children for the welfare state.

What liberals call income inequality, I call not-willing-to-work equally. The non-workers' motto has become, "Why would I get a job when you do the work for me?"

The United States government does not understand the separation of religion and law. The lower courts do not understand the separation of religion and law. Even the Supreme Court of the United States does not understand the separation of religion and law. This is because all of these establishments have been dumbed down as to what religion is and is not, or we would not have the welfare state destroying the United States.

It is my opinion that if the liberal progressives had not interfered with the National Charity Organization in 1935 through the Social Security Act, religion would have had eighty-five years to fine tune the Charity Organization Societies, and they would have become far better than anyone could ever imagine. This is because we would have a national church separate from a national government. Unlike the national government, a national church could invest and make a profit, and it could also save.

Investing and saving are two very important features in the religious model. In 2019, Americans donated $427 billion to US charities; in 2018, they gave $410 billion, even after paying $2 trillion in taxes.

In two years, Americans gave $837 billion. If they had consolidated these funds to a single point with a national church for two years, the church could invest in real estate, businesses, and commodities, creating its own cash flow.

Now, if Americans continued tithing at just $427 billion per year to a single point, and the church had built a cash flow to pay for its executives and workers while saving for five years, the result would equal $2 trillion.

And it would <u>still be your money</u>, unlike when you trust the government with your money, where you give one year and the money is gone. Paying tithes to the church would simply be Americans investing in Americans.

Whenever it comes to the point where the church can financially take over welfare spending, we will not be paying $2 trillion in welfare taxation that increases every year.

Now, let us revisit the Joint Economic Committee projections:

- When government stops spending $2 trillion, <u>66 million</u> **children** will come out of poverty.
- When government stops spending $2 trillion, the **economy** will increase by $760 billion. Over seven years, this increases to $4 trillion, 900 billion.
- When government stops spending $2 trillion, it will increase **wages** by $520 billion. Over seven years, this increases to $3 trillion, 360 billion.
- When government stops spending $2 trillion, it will increase **workers'** yearly income by $17,900.[56]

Political pundits have determined that if the United States would merely come to a sane level of taxation, all the businesses

---

[56] Joint Economic Committee Study 1-5, Jim Saxton, Vice chairman, 1996.

that have left the country for tax reasons would return to the US, bringing an estimated $7 trillion back to the economy.

Soon, Americans would gain confidence in the national church, then the religious would have a national voice, thus setting the standard of the nation by God's standard to give life and give life more abundantly. Further, we would have a national financial institution to carry out policies that we deem most likely to accomplish our happiness at the national level.

This change would prevent what is occurring in the government now, as every state is pulling the government in a different direction; an action that is dividing our nation and our government.

Separation Of Church And
State In The Kingdom Of God

I n Matthew 8:20, Jesus said, "The foxes have holes, and the birds of the air have nests: but the son of man has no place to lay his head." Jesus said this because the religious leaders, as well as the officers of the law, occupied the temple, making it a kingdom of this world.

Jesus was a thorn in the side of the Jews, as His disciples openly said that He was the King of the Jews, which threatened their power over their church-state. This can be seen in the trial of Jesus.

John recorded Jesus's trial in the book of John. In John 11:49, we read that the high priest had called on the officers of the law for Jesus's death, yet the officers of the law could not find Him. In John 11:57, the high priest said that if any man knew where Jesus was, he should show it. Then, in John 18:3, Judas had received a band of men and officers from the Chief Priest Caiaphas and had taken thirty pieces of silver from the high priest, betraying Jesus unto the hands of the high priest (John 18:12).

John 18:19 says that the high priest asked Jesus of His disciples and of His doctrine. In John 19:20, Jesus answered, "I spoke openly to the world, I always taught in the synagogue and in the temple, and in secret I have said nothing." Then, in John 19:21,

47

He says, "Why do you ask me? Ask them which heard me, they know what I said."

In John 18:22, we see the officers of the law in cahoots with the high priest. This is due to the lack of separation of church and state; the officer who stood by slapped Jesus with the palm of his hand, saying, "How dare you answer the high priest so."

Then John 18:28 states that the high priest and the officers took Jesus from Caiaphas to the "hall of judgment." Today, this would be known as the criminal court. John 18:30 tells us that when the court was in session, Pilate, a criminal court judge, said, "What accusation bring you against this man?"

They answered him in John 18:30, saying, "He is a criminal, or we would not have brought him to you." This response did not answer Pilate's question of what criminal charge they accused Jesus of that would be worthy of scourging or death.

Pilate, being a judge of the criminal court, determined that they had no criminal charge against Jesus, except to call Him a criminal. Then, in John 18:31, Pilate said to the accusers, "Take him and judge him according to your law." But they said, "It is not lawful for us to put him to death."

As a judge, Pilate went to the accused Jesus in John 18:33, asking Him, "Are you the King of the Jews?" In John 18:34, Jesus basically answered Pilate, saying, "Did you know this yourself or did someone tell you I was?" Jesus knew the priest had brought Him there because He threatened their power, as He was the true king, having authority over the priests.

Then, in John 18:35, Pilate, speaking as a judge to the accused, said, "Your own nation and the chief priests have delivered you to me: What have you done?"

In John 18:36, Jesus cleverly said, "My kingdom is not of this world," inasmuch confirming that His nation had no separation of church and state, and that was not His kingdom. Jesus said this knowing that Leviticus, of which He is king, is not Deuteronomy, as they are separate.

Jesus continued, saying, "If my kingdom were of this world then my servants would fight." The worldly kingdoms of His time had no separation of church and state; and if His kingdom were of this world, He would use the power of the state and fight so He would not be delivered to the Jews. He ended by saying, "But now my kingdom is not from here" (John 18:36).

Then, in John 18:37, Pilate said to Jesus, "Are you a king then?" Jesus responded, clearing up the previous parable in which He spoke of the kingdom, saying, "You just said I was a king. To this end I was born, and for this reason I came into this world, that I should bear witness to the truth."

The truth Jesus was referring to is that He is the king of Leviticus, where the high priests should have known the truth by the Covenant of God—that Leviticus is separate from the law of Deuteronomy.

Pilate again returned to the accusers in John 18:38, saying, "I find no fault in him at all, and tried to make release for him but they would not have it, because they knew the officers would be removed from the temple and the priest would be subject to his authority."

So then, in John 19:1-5, Pilate took Jesus and had him scourged to appease the high priest and the officers of the law. He then put on Jesus a crown of thorns and a purple robe, which was a sign of royalty. Pilate returned to the accusers, telling them, "I bring him forth so you may know I find no fault in him." He brought Jesus out wearing the crown of thorns and purple robe.

Then, in John 19:6, when the chief priests (church) and the officers (state) saw Jesus dressed as a king who could take away their power, they went into full-blown murder mode, screaming,

"Crucify him, crucify him!" But Pilate said, "You crucify him, for I find no fault in him."

In John 19:7, the Jews answered Pilate, saying, "We have a law, and by our law, he ought to die, because he made himself the Son of God."

A few moments earlier, in John 18:31, the Jews had just said that it was not lawful for them to put Jesus to death. Now, they are saying that there is a law and that Jesus should die by the hand of the law for religious reasons. In other words, he was killed because there was no separation of church and state.

One can only wonder if the Jews knew the Scripture, and by the Scripture, they knew a king would come and take them out of their places, so they made a law that allowed them to kill the Son of God when He came to earth.

Jesus spoke of this exact moment in the parable of the vineyard in Luke 20:9-15, where God sent His servant to collect the tithe and they beat him; He sent a second, and they beat him, followed by a third, whom they wounded also. Then the lord of the vineyard asked, "What shall I do? I will send my beloved Son: it may be that they will reverence him when they see him." But when the husbandmen saw him, they reasoned among themselves, saying, "This is the heir: come, let us kill him, that the inheritance may be ours." So they cast him out of the vineyard and killed him.

Hope For The Future

urge all conservatives and religious people to consider these matters carefully. Contemplate the fact that when America elected Barak Obama as president, we were all looking for change because we could sense the need for change.

God gave us President Barak, knowing that he would double down on the church-state. God let Barak's presidency happen so we could be taken to the brink of terror when his administration launched an all-out assault on Christians and conservatives, calling us bitter clingers clinging to our guns and Bibles on national television. Our God-given rights were disrespected, and these rights echo the biblical rights.

Obama used the power of the IRS to assault our conservative religious beliefs, our finances, and our children's futures. He unjustly militarized the Department of Justice, refusing to stop the violence of acorn, Black Lives Matter, and others against us.

His actions during his presidency were so bad that they sparked a nationwide prayer rally where we prayed for God to help us and not give us Hillary Clinton as our next president. God's plan to let us have what we wanted worked; be careful what you ask for because God is going to give it to you.

We prayed for relief, and as we prayed, we saw the entrance of twenty-five candidates. I will never forget what I saw in that election field—outright socialism, threats from all sides swearing to relieve us of our First Amendment rights and Second Amendment rights.

God heard our prayers, but because it was hard for us to make a unanimous decision, God Himself made the decision. He knew Trump was a warrior and probably the only one who could handle the oncoming assault from the left. Anybody else would have crumbled under this four-year, minute-by-minute assault. I liked Ted Cruz because he serves the state I live in, but looking back, the liberals who tried to impeach President Trump would have destroyed him; he just about lost his composure when Trump called him "Lying Ted" and made pretty harsh statements about his wife.

And I'll never forget seeing Trump lambast all twenty-four candidates left and right, leaving them behind like they were going in reverse as he propelled forward.

God is trying to help us, and He knows what is best for us. His Word says, "For I know the thoughts I think toward you saith the Lord, thoughts of peace, and not of evil to give you an expected end" (Jer. 29:11).

Throughout this book, I have done my best to tell you the things God has told me through the Spirit of His Word.

I have shown you that the founders established this great nation on the Covenant of God.

I have shown you how the laws the founders made in the First Amendment make it possible to end the liberal destruction of our nation.

I have shown you, with proof by government documents, that what has happened is true.

I have shown you God's economics that no nation has seen before.

Like a jigsaw puzzle, the pieces fit perfectly together to form the kingdom of God.

Now, I would like to show you a door named peace: on the other side is life, liberty, and happiness. Together, we can walk through this door and establish the kingdom God has prepared for us from the foundation of the world.

> *Ask and it shall be given to you,*
> *seek and you shall find,*
> *knock and it shall be opened to you.*[57]

If you decide to follow God's way, it will end the liberal assault on our country and raise a standard of peace that the world has never known. It won't be easy, but we will have God on our side. If you have read the Bible, you know that we win this war.

God has endowed mankind with certain unalienable rights. Among these are life, liberty, and the pursuit of happiness, but also the right to worship God, to follow His way, and to choose His form of government that is most likely to affect our safety and happiness. In the Declaration of Independence, our nation's founders stated that governments are instituted among men deriving their just powers from the consent of the governed; that whenever <u>any form of government</u> becomes destructive to these ends, it is the right of the governed to alter or abolish it.

The governed have not consented to the government the *unjust* powers of establishing a religious government. No matter what you call it, care for the poor is care for the poor and has been the religious duty since Exodus 23:11, where 3,400 years ago, God instructed us to take on this duty.

For the first time in 3,400 years, God has openly revealed to mankind His will to establish the kingdom of God. There is no new land to flee to; therefore, we must stand for God.

---

[57] Matthew 7:7

Leviticus is our religion; this book of the Bible was written for the priests, and God wants a nation of priests. Jesus is the king of Leviticus. He is the High Priest, God's administer of welfare, healthcare, education, and housing and urban development, as rendered in Matthew 25:31-46.

I stand on my argument; the welfare state is the unconstitutional establishment of the Judeo-Christian religion's charity. It violates the First Amendment by being a law made by Congress that establishes charity and prohibits the free exercise thereof.

I'm just a man; I make mistakes, and there may be a few in this book, but overall, I have learned from many sources that the liberal wing of the Democrat party established Christian charity, and that the Constitution's First Amendment and God's Word could stop them from destroying the United States.

The founders of the United States gave us a toolbox for enforcing our right to freedom of religion in the First Amendment:

The freedom from laws respecting an **establishment** of religion.

The freedom from laws, which prohibit the **free exercise** of religion.

The freedom of **speech** to protest an unconstitutional establishment of religion.

The freedom of the **press** to expose it to the **court of public opinion.**

The freedom to peaceably **assemble** to work out a plan of action.

The freedom to **petition** government for redress of our grievances.

The first question is, do we believe it? There are a lot of new concepts and discoveries here of which we have never heard. Hopefully, I have presented enough evidence to answer the question: is welfare, healthcare, education, and housing truly Christian charity?

I presented GuideStar to show a reliable, trusted source of religious information that lists 493,970 organizations. If there were only two people running each organization, there would be a million people who agree that welfare, healthcare, education, and housing are truly Christian charity.

The next question would be, did government really establish welfare, healthcare, education, and housing from Christian charity? For this question, I presented evidence from an expert in history, Professor Theron Schlabach from Goshen College. The list of records he used is one million pages or more, located at the Social Security Administration archive. Evidently, the people at the Social Security Administration believed the Social Security Act established charity, because they suppressed it from public view from 1969 until 2001, in violation of the Freedom of Information Act of 1966.

This brings us to the following question: does the government's establishment of welfare, healthcare, education, and housing from Christian charity really violate the First Amendment? I mean, they didn't actually start a government church.

Although the Social Security Act was found unconstitutional on many other grounds, most of the court's First Amendment challenges were based on tax status. Everson v. Board of Education 330 US 1 (1947) developed the first consistent test for an establishment clause challenge. "The statute must have a secular legislative purpose." A statute is a law made by Congress, and under this test, if the statute has a religious purpose, it would fail the test. Being the path to salvation, as Jesus Christ prescribed, and the establishment of Leviticus for the priests and the miracles of God and Jesus Christ, you could safely say that it would be impossible, under any circumstance, for these statutes to be secular.

The next question would be, has it caused us damage? I ask this simply because the courts will rarely grant relief if there are no damages. For this question, I show evidence from the Joint Economic Committee. These reports go directly to Congress and make them aware of the damages caused by the legislation they have created.

In the present situation, I would suggest we start with exercising our freedom to **assemble** to discuss the argument and come to a full understanding of the issues before we make plans to protest against it, or petition government for redress of grievances.

Finally, we must all fully understand the argument, come to an agreement on a plan of action, and proceed to the next tool in the toolbox.

I plan to use the **press** to expose the truth to the court of public opinion and try to persuade every conservative and religious grassroots organization to lobby government, making them aware of these findings and our demands that the welfare state is unconstitutional, as well as informing them of the need to cease and desist the enforcement of the Social Security Act, the Affordable Healthcare Act, the Education Act, and the Housing and Urban Development Act.

Then I will give them a chance to respond with a counter argument and debate their argument, giving them the chance to debate argument versus argument by preponderance of evidence.

Then, if it cannot be resolved without involving the law, as a last resort, we would re-assemble and debate our last option to petition government for redress of grievances by filing a class action lawsuit for relief, demanding the court to issue an injunction to cease and desist all activity in the Social Security Act, the Affordable Healthcare Act, the Education Act, and the Housing and Urban Development Act, and to declare these acts unconstitutional.

We must repent and obey the Covenant, and, as the body of Christ, we must come out of the world and enter into the kingdom of God.

"The time is fulfilled, and the kingdom of God is at hand. Repent ye and believe the gospel."[58]

---

[58] Mark 1:15

www.ingramcontent.com/pod-product-compliance
Lightning Source LLC
Chambersburg PA
CBHW050515290526
45786CB00007B/2581